VAN GOGH

By: ALBERTO MARTINI

AVENEL BOOKS

NEW YORK

Library of Congress Cataloging in Publication Data
Gogh, Vincent van, 1853-1890.
Van Gogh.
1. Gogh, Vincent van, 1853-1890. I. Martini, Alberto.
ND653.G7A4 1978 759.9492 78-59677
ISBN 0-517-24953-7

"...it is often difficult to understand what encloses us, what walls us up, what seems to bury us, but, nevertheless, we feel undefined bars, gates, walls."

Van Gogh spent his life struggling to find peace of mind and soul by making larger-than-life efforts to bring succor and love to his fellow-men. It was a struggle that the poor, driven artist was never to win, and he was to lead a life of mental torment and physical pain until he died, at 37, with a bullet in his heart.

He was born on March 30, 1853, at Groot Zundert, a village in Dutch Brabant. And with the encouragements of his clergyman Father, Vincent began working at 16 as an art dealer. He was first employed at the Goupil Gallery branch that had been founded by an uncle at the Hague. He remained there for three years (1869-1873) before transferring to a more important branch in London (1873-1875), and finally to the main office in Paris.

Van Gogh developed a passion for the paintings of the old and new masters that he studied in museums and in art galleries. He lost interest in his job as an art-dealer and returned home unexpectedly at the beginning of 1876. He still did not know what he wanted to do, but he read a great deal, he drew, and often submerged himself in intense religious moods. From then on, his life became that of a perpetual wanderer who carried his anguish and his desire for inner peace wherever he went. At Ramsgate, in Kent, he became a language teacher; at Isleworth, near London, he was an assistant preacher. He was a clerk in a bookshop at Dordrecht, and a theology student in Amsterdam. In Brussels, he attended seminars for clergymen. Van Gogh was appointed travelling minister in the coal fields of the Borinage in January 1879.

It was there, as he wrote in letters to his brother Theo, that he attended free courses at the great university of misery, sharing the hardships and the privations of the miners, to the extent of destroying his health, both physical and mental. It was a desperate tug-of-war between his exhausted physical strength and his moral energy from which he emerged with a nervous breakdown, a crisis from which he never truly recovered. After an intense period of self-examination during the summer of 1880 in the Borinage, he discovered his vocation and his destiny in painting. He described this moment of self-discovery in a letter to his brother Theo, who remained devoted to Vincent all his life and never failed to offer moral and economic support in moments of crisis.

Van Gogh's development as an artist was as irregular and stormy as his preparation for the ministry. He left the Borinage where he had filled notebooks with drawings that captured the desperate lives of the miners and went to Brussels to study anatomy and perspective. From there, he moved into the new family home at Etten where he encountered firm opposition to his artistic endeavors. There he was disappointed in his love for a widowed cousin. It was a second rejection, his first going back to 1874, in London. In the winter of 1881, at the Hague, Vincent began his first paintings under the guidance of another cousin, Mauve. During this period the 29-year old shared his already difficult life with Christine, a prostitute, but he was forced to abandon her because of his extreme poverty.

He rejoined his family the winter of 1883 in Neunen where they had moved a little earlier. Vincent worked intensely at Neunen for about two years. Here, tragedy touched his life. He proposed to a neighbor, Margot Begemann, who had professed great love for him. Her parents refused their permission and she tried to commit suicide.

Then Van Gogh was forced by his father's sudden death and an overwhelming need for money to move to Antwerp during the winter of 1885-1886, and later to Paris, where he joined his brother Theo. In the two years that he spent in Paris, his cultural experiences created a basis for those extraordinary artistic achievements of the following period. He took lessons at Cormon's studio where he met other young painters such as Toulouse-Lautrec and Emile Bernard. He participated in the animated discussions that followed the outburst of Impressionism. He took sides with the Pointillists and the Synthesists, and met such artists as Pissaro, Seurat, Signac and Gauguin. He felt himself closest to Gauguin. When he left for Arles to paint, he begged his friend to join him. Gauguin arrived on October 20, 1888 and the two months that followed were very productive for both. But the differences in their personalities and continual discussions began to wear down Van Gogh's fragile nerves. On the night of December 23, he attacked Gauguin twice with a razor, and then, to punish himself, he turned the weapon against himself and cut off his ear, carefully wrapped it up, and brought it to a girl in a brothel.

This was the first of a series of violent crises that were to plague him during his last years. In May 1889, at 36, he was admitted to the asylum of Saint-Remy-de-Provence in order to undergo intensive treatment, but his health continued to deteriorate. A year later, he went to Auvers-sur-Oise, where Dr. Gachet accepted him as a patient. On the way to Auvers, Van Gogh stopped briefly at his brother's house in Paris.

Although he appeared reasonably calm on the surface, the final outburst was near. Two months after his arrival in Auvers, on July 27, on a pleasant day in the open country, he suffered a final crisis and shot himself in the heart with a revolver. He died two days later in the presence of Theo and of his friend Gachet.

3

"Death in the life of an artist is not perhaps the most difficult thing."

The Postman Roulin—Winterthur Collection, H. Hanloser

"Everyone claims the right to dream, the right to graze in the fields of azure, the right to be spirited towards the stars when denied Absolute Truth. . . . No painter or sculptor worthy of the name can ever be satisfied by the myopic imitation of social intercourse, the stupid imitation of the Nature's excesses, the unimaginative observation, the optical deceit, the glory of being so faithful, so trivially exact as a daguerreotype." These words were written by the young poet Albert Aurier, one of the few people who appreciated the work of Van Gogh during his life, and the only one who wrote a great deal about him. Aurier summarizes the French artistic climate around the year 1892, in the flourishing period of the Symbolists.

With Gauguin, Redon, Seurat and Lautrec, the major figures of the post-Impressionist movement, Van Gogh had a distinctive and certainly prominent role. He too, was a visionary primarily concerned with penetrating the labyrinth of his soul and reaching the Absolute that lay beyond the shifting appearances of the world and its objects. But his imagination never reflected an abstract desire for evasion. It was rather an investigation of reality on which he focused; a reality to which Vincent, the simple name with which he signed his paintings and by which he was known in the Parisian art circles, felt attracted.

He was drawn to an awareness of the world that was inside and around him, to the terrible passions disturbing the serenity of his soul, to a sun rotating menacingly overhead, to olive trees twisting in a mute suffering, to cypress trees becoming somber flames of desperation. But this was the only world possible for a man who lived and thought, who suffered and dreamed on this earth. Above him were the stars, and Vincent reached up to them for salvation. And down here on the earth were the flowers and the wheat. Even during those moments of anguish, he felt that nature continued its vital cycles of birth and regeneration.

"I prefer a melancholy that aspires and searches, to a melancholy that is stagnant and mournful, and that leads to desperation" wrote Van Gogh. He accepted the turbulent condition of his spirit with a heroic will. He was conscious of having at every moment to overcome his anguish in order to create a work that would be more than just a passive mirror of his despair. His paintings do not imply the drama of a defeat, or a metaphisical malediction; rather they express a feverish tension, the sign of a desperate internal struggle which is brought out into the open. It can be said that each of his paintings presents a way to live and to act, a method which allows him to communicate with the world and humanity. This contrasts with Van Gogh's naive life as a mystic, but is fully realized through the authority of his genius in his paintings. It can be added that each of his paintings is the form of a tangible reality. Simultaneously, it is the concrete image of his inner reality, a total identification and absoluteness that annihilates any intellectual preconception. Reality, for Van Gogh, is only a pretext to express a subjective state of being, not something that is borrowed and distorted at one's will in order to exalt the overwhelming flames of passion. Reality confronts us with a reflection of one's self, a semblance of our own vision. This was perhaps why Van Gogh was only able to work with real objects, for he knew at this point that the external world, once placed in a particular light and a specific color, was the emotional equivalent of his inner world.

A poetical attitude of that kind undoubtedly originated from the assumptions of the Symbolist movement. It demanded an absolute sincerity, and rejected a reliance on traditional conventions. The artist was alone, he had daily to find a solution for his problems of expression. Vincent was conscious of the difficulty of his undertaking. Yet, he countered this with a passion and a courage astonishing in a person racked with emotional problems. He lacerated every mask that hid his soul, he destroyed every symbolic and literary metaphor in order to reveal his inner being. Each of his paintings is a page of an illustrated journal in which the story of his spirit is delineated with its hopes and disappointments, its anguish and enlightenment. At first his mental state made him occasionally tear out a page, but little by little, even weeks and months are missing in this journal. Still many lucid masterpieces remain and constitute the glory of Vincent Van Gogh, painter and poet.

Until he produced his best works in his last years, Vincent went through a long period of laborious study and incertitude. As a boy, he already liked to draw houses and landscapes in the Dutch style; it was not yet a real passion for painting, but rather an interest he developed during his apprenticeship as an art-dealer in the Hague, in London and Paris. Later, with those impulses of generosity that were typical of his mystical nature, he threw himself into a humanitarian and religious mission. It was a bitter failure, as we know, but during those years passed in the coal fields of the Borinage, he discovered the real path, and for the first time gave himself entirely to painting.

Drawing was for him a different way of accomplishing his humanitarian mission, a way that witnessed the work and misery of the miners, a personal action completed alone on a piece of paper, as if it were a prayer. Millet was his ideal master, the real modern painter. He opened, Van Gogh wrote, "distant expectations". Among the old masters, Rembrandt and Frans Hals were his favorites. Van Gogh emphasized the human rather than the stylistic elements. His eyes looked out on the world and on painting with an interest turned more to emotions than to a representation of reality. The drawings of this period are technically unsatisfactory showing a completely amateurish roughness in the outlines and shadings. Vincent was the first to recognize it, and he felt the need for more serious and profound studies. His cousin Mauve, a good painter of the Hague school, helped him with advice and suggestions, and introduced him to the artistic circles of the city. But Mauve was unable to impose a sense of discipline and application on his impatient student.

Van Gogh's first paintings are dated from the year 1882. Up to that time he had limited himself to drawings. These paintings reveal the influence of the Dutch school of realism and a clear interest for chiaroscuro, textured pigments and incrusted impasto of colors. What is still missing in these paintings is a controlled technique. His watercolors are freer, more immediate. They can express the complex spatial structures of the landscapes by using bold surface planes. In his drawings, along with typical popular motifs, Van Gogh tried to present symbolic themes derived from contemporary English prints.

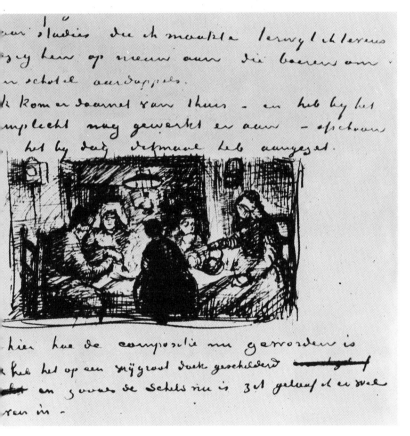

The Potato Eaters—Drawing in pen and ink. From a letter to his brother Theo.

During his stay in Neunen, from the end of 1883 to the end of 1885, Van Gogh concentrated on themes of earth and labor. In these simple works, there is no sign of naivete, but instead a will to express an emotional content that was intimately connected to the hard life of the peasants and workers of his country with distorted lines, bituminous materials, violent brushstrokes and elementary contrasts of shadow and light. The *Potato Eaters,* from the V. W. Van Gogh Collection at Laren (now in the National Museum Vincent Van Gogh in Amsterdam), is the most important painting of this series. In this work, the artist has fully realized his social and moral intentions: hands deformed by labor, bony and lined faces so cruelly revealed by vibrant brushstrokes. But at the same time, these paintings denounce the limit of an experience which could not be further developed. Van Gogh wanted to be truly Dutch, he wanted to remake Rembrandt and Hals, he ignored the painters that Theo enthusiastically wrote about from Paris. Having finished the painting into which he threw all his energy, Van Gogh felt that he was at a dead end, that he had to question everything.

In his letters of October 1885, Van Gogh often commented on the qualities of expression of color. During the winter of 1885-1886, in Antwerp, he discovered Japanese prints and subsequently was drawn to color. Theo was now writing about the paintings of the Paris avant-garde, the colors of which shone with solar clarity. These letters began to assume a different weight in Vincent's mind. At that point, he felt the need to abandon his former position. His trip to Paris was the inevitable result of this cultural crisis. Van Gogh arrived in the French capital in the first days of March 1886, and it was in Paris that his painting went through a renaissance. Van Gogh was thirty-three years old and he had to start all over again.

First, he painted some still lives, where, influenced by Monticelli, he experimented again with thick pigments and impasto. But afterwards, he definitively liberated himself from any residue of traditional painting. This did not happen because of the proximity of the Impressionist milieu, but as a consequence of the influence of the "Plein air" school and of the discussions and innovating proposals of a group of artists who were committed to go beyond the

Harvest at Arles—Basel, Private Collection.

problems of verisimilitude. There were the Divisionists on the one hand, who attempted to systematize the lyrical improvisations of Monet and Renoir in proposing a plastic and spatial reconstruction of a painting by using short brushstrokes of color; these were divided on the canvas, but were ultimately recomposed on the retina. On the other hand, there were the Synthesists, Emile Bernard and Paul Gauguin, who organized a painting with color planes which were free of any descriptive or naturalistic function, adding symbolic and literary meanings to the subject.

Vincent did not join these movements they were so extraneous to his personality. He could not accept the excesses of the Divisionist rules, and he rejected the Synthesists' intellectualism, that favored an escape from reality. He took what was useful to him from both sides, the arbitrary colors of the Synthesists, and the use of the fragmented, at times minute, brushstrokes of the Divisionists.

In addition to the influence of these contemporary art movements, one must also take into account Van Gogh's renewed enthusiasm for the Japanese prints that had covered the walls of his room in Antwerp. In Paris, the prints were taken off the walls and made an integral part of his paintings, appearing in the background of several of his portraits. While Van Gogh's relationship with oriental art was a difficult one, it nevertheless remained a major influence. The prints of Hokusai, Hiroshige and Utamaro were the most readily accessible in Paris in those years, they were exhibited at the Bing Gallery and represented for Vincent something very different from his temperament; an irretrievably lost paradise of a joyful and serene art, freed from any touch of passion. Most significantly, they revealed a style which was exclusively committed to color and line, a relationship that defined space and atmosphere, form and light, exposing the total absence of chiaroscuro in their pictorial language. While he admired these prints and wanted to recreate their lyrical and meditative style, Van Gogh found that he had to consider again the problems that had preoccupied him during the years in the Hague and in Neunen. These prints influenced some of Van Gogh's luminous landscapes of the end of 1886 and the beginning of 1887 as well as the drawings executed with small dashes and points which suggested depth and translated an emotional solar chromatism in graphical terms.

In 1887, Vincent, still taken by his Japanese passion, began to adopt the Pointillist technique, noticing how the small brushstrokes of color increased the luminosity of a painting. He rejected the systematic rigor of Seurat and Signac. But he felt closer to the latter and when in the presence of his more descriptive paintings, he was unable to overcome a state of excitement which he felt marked the authenticity of his feelings.

Even among the Pointillist group he remained isolated, as he did not wish to appear like a student, who had only learned half of his lesson, in front of his companions. He only occasionally used the divided spots of color, preferring to bring out the impetuosity of the pigments by using vigorous brushstrokes, which clashed, but harmoniously recomposed themselves with violence and energy. In the fall, but more precisely during the winter of 1887-1888, this experience came to an end.

Van Gogh began to develope a new language, a brushstroke which drew and constructed an image with a freedom and immediacy that evoked the forms and spaces of an almost vertiginous vibration, a brushstroke which followed the feverish rhythm of a desperately tense soul, from the heights of exaltations to the depths of despair.

Innumerable discussions had in the end worn out Van Gogh's fragile nerves; he was also disappointed by his inability to combine the most creative forces of those exciting years of Parisian life. After having benefited from these varied stimulations, Van Gogh felt the need to withdraw to a quiet place in order to work and gather all his experiences together. He chose Provence, and on February 21, arrived and settled in Arles.

The works of the first months were not so very different from those of the Parisian period, but with the oncoming of the summer, his colors became more intense, to the point of brilliance. It was the happy result of a process which had begun months before in the second version of the portrait of Tanguy (Paris, Niarchos Coll.), and it was the beginning of an extraordinary period which was to continue through the last two years of the artist's life. The conscious decision that led him to choose arbitrary colors and to distort shapes was now resolved in a burning sense of immediacy. From then on, whenever he had to place himself in

Au Charbonnage—Amsterdam, National Museum Vincent Van Gogh.

different color planes, but this did not interfere with the nature of his problem of expression. In fact, several paintings of this period have a luminous intensity that border on the hallucinatory, and he was never able to equal that intensity again.

After the tragic crisis that unleashed the quarrel with Gauguin, Van Gogh lived his saddest days, and this is reflected in his work. Periods of almost frenetic activity were followed by days of total depression. The forced confinement in the hospital in Arles, the result of a petition by some of his neighbors, was his hardest blow. He no longer had any faith in himself. He was afraid of a relapse, and finally he went into voluntary isolation at the asylum in Saint-Remy. The only life that was left to him was his work. The one hundred and fifty paintings that he made during the year of his recovery are a sign of his desperate cry for life. When his illness allowed him to work, Vincent confessed on the canvas the inexhaustible vitality of his spirit, the anguish that filled his vision and his rare moments of confidence. The brushstrokes became a violent symbol which twisted and distended itself with the rhythm of his emotions. Nature became to him a spectacle of disasters.

In May 1890, Van Gogh made a courageous decision and broke away from his isolation at Saint-Remy. He moved to Auvers-sur-Oise, where Dr. Gachet, himself a painter and friend of Cezanne and Pissaro, was willing to take care of him. Outside of the hallucinatory atmosphere of the asylum, the artist passed a relatively happy period. His work reflects moments of tranquility and sympathy toward the world. But it was only an illusory calm, all too often interrupted by violent explosions, in which he relieved his tension with screams.

On a sunny Sunday in July, when the wheat was yellow and the sky bluer than usual, when the black crows flew away in fright, just like the painting he had completed that very month, Van Gogh ended his troubled days with a shot from a revolver.

It was a tragic end to a short life, consumed by excessive and strong passions. But it marked the beginning of his "success". Many artists, from the Fauves to the Expressionists followed in his wake. And the masters of our century continue to study a man whose masterworks reflect the brilliance, fire, passion and intensity of a tortured soul.

front of the simplest or most insignificant men or objects, Van Gogh immediately felt their passions and emotions. The greatness of Van Gogh lay precisely there. He had broken down all the mental barriers that separated him from reality and was therefore able to communicate his inner vision of reality through his sufferings.

Gauguin's arrival in Arles created doubts in Vincent's vision. On some occasions, Van Gogh tried to construct paintings by using

Index of the illustrations

I - Girl in White in the Woods - Otterlo, Kröller-Müller Stichting - *This painting goes back to August 1882, and is part of Van Gogh's first works after his intense experience as a preacher, in 1879-80, in one of the most depressed areas of Belgium. He made this painting during a very serene period at his father's house, where he immersed himself in the contemplation of the landscape and nature.*

II - Fisherman on the Beach - Otterlo, Kröller-Müller Stichting - *Van Gogh painted this canvas during his stay in the Dutch province of Drenthe in 1883. This region had a great fascination for the artist who was struck not only by the landscape, but by the life of the humble, toward whom he felt an instinctive commitment of solidarity and brotherhood.*

III - Peasant Plowing and Peasant Woman - Wuppertal, Museum Von der Heydt - *Toward the end of 1883 Van Gogh returned to his family at the small village of Nuenen where he began the first series of paintings that would be fundamental to his artistic evolution. He refused to paint what was conventionally held to be beautiful, but sought the more modest images of the toilers of the earth.*

IV - Still Life with Five Bottles and a Bowl - Otterlo, Kröller-Müller Stichting - *This painting goes back to the Nuenen period of 1884-85, when Van Gogh sought the barest and most essential elements of things. He painted the simplest and most modest objects that reflected the peasant's world. These represented to him the most sacred values of existence.*

V - Peasant Woman Sweeping - Otterlo, Kröller-Müller Stichting - *During the years 1884-85, Van Gogh's expressive researches found one of their most fruitful and intense periods. He painted many figures of peasants in their most varied attitudes, such as this one, as well as the humble world of village craftsmen, and various still lifes.*

VI - The Potato Eaters - Otterlo, Kröller-Müller Stichting - *This was an important subject for Van Gogh, who made three different versions (this is the second, of April 1885), as well as various drawings and studies, among them a sketch in a letter to his brother which is now at the National Museum Vincent Van Gogh in Amsterdam.*

VII - Head of a Peasant Woman with a White Cap - Otterlo, Kröller-Müller Stichting - *This is a study for the third version of The Potato Eaters made in May 1885. One can see how Van Gogh's creative expression had reached a very high level: the grossness of the faces expresses the life, the misery, and the drama of the existence of these people.*

VIII - The Potato Eaters - Amsterdam, National Museum Vincent Van Gogh - *The third version of this subject, begun in April 1885, is a testimony to the lengthy research for a highly original technique that permitted Van Gogh to reduce his colors to tonalities of bister, brown and bitumen, broken up by brushstrokes of white, to correspond to the atmosphere of the world that he depicted.*

IX - The Potato Eaters - (detail) - Amsterdam, National Museum Vincent Van Gogh - *This third version was finished in May 1885, and it ended Van Gogh's formative phase and his dominating interest in the materially dense chiaroscuro that he perfected during his stay at Nuenen. His love for the earth and its toilers is fully expressed in this painting.*

X - The Quay at Antwerp - Amsterdam, National Museum Vincent Van Gogh - *Van Gogh's brief stay in Antwerp at the end of 1885, after having left the village of Nuenen, marked an important step in his artistic evolution. In this first painting of the period one can already detect his search for a vaster scale of colors and a greater luminosity.*

XI - Bathing-Barge on the Oise at Asnières - Upperville, Va., from the collection of Mr. and Mrs. Paul Mellon - *This canvas, painted during the summer of 1887 after Van Gogh had been in Paris for over one year, bears witness to the enormous influence that the Parisian culture — and the city — had on the painter. The lessons of the impressionists, with whom he was closely associated, are evident.*

XII - View of Paris from Montmartre - Basel, Öffentliche Kunstsammlung - *Van Gogh was always fascinated by his surroundings. In Paris he explored the streets, the houses, the gardens, the roofs of his quarter of the city. To capture the luminous atmosphere of the Parisian suburb he lightened the tone of his colors. This painting was done in the fall of 1886, when he had already met Pissarro.*

XIII - Le Moulin de la Galette - Buenos Aires, Museo Nacional de Bellas Artes - *The Montmartre quarter was the section of Paris that most attracted Van Gogh: its windmills evoked scenes from his childhood. He made several paintings of the mill, expressing and comparing his own experiences with those of his friends of the period of 1886-87, Lautrec and Signac.*

XIV - Le Moulin de la Galette - Otterlo, Kröller-Müller Stichting - *This painting of Montmartre is of 1886. Daily Van Gogh exchanged ideas with friends who were part of the impressionist, divisionist and synthesist movements, but their concepts had no influence on his totally instinctive way of expressing emotion. In this painting the brushwork is vigorous and dense, far removed from the prevailing artistic rules of the period.*

XV - Le Moulin de la Galette - Pittsburgh, Museum of Art, Carnegie Institute - *In March 1887, when he finished this canvas, Van Gogh had met Gauguin and Seurat. He had absorbed from both of these painters the researches of synthesism and divisionism, adapting them to his own needs. The brushstrokes are often separated, but without any sense of affectation, and the color is never symbolically abstract.*

XVI - Interior of a Restaurant - Otterlo, Kröller-Müller Stichting - *Every new experience, every new technique and theory were valid occasions for Van Gogh to enrich his palette and his pictorial capabilities, but without ever abandoning his originality, which was free of any preconceived scheme. The pointillism of this painting reflects his continual search for an expressive synthesis.*

XVII - Seated Woman at the "Café du Tambourin" - Amsterdam, National Museum Vincent Van Gogh - *An unusual factor of this painting of February 1887 is that there is a similar one by Toulouse-Lautrec portraying the same woman in the same pose. Note how the two painters, of such different artistic training and temperament, treated this subject with a similar sensitivity.*

XVIII - Portrait of a Young Woman in Profile - U.S.A., private collection - *Rarely has an artist paid so much attention to nature and human beings as Van Gogh, who was irresistibly attracted by the landscape and his surroundings as well as by human faces. He wrote that he preferred, "to paint the eyes of men rather than cathedrals."*

XIX - Reclining Female Nude - France, private collection - *This painting, made during the summer of 1887, testifies to the productivity of Van Gogh's two years in Paris. The nude was never a frequent theme in his artistic production, but from the encounters and experiences of this period there emerged the most varied works, some of which were just phases of his artistic evolution, and others authentic masterpieces.*

XX - Self-Portrait - Amsterdam, National Museum Van Gogh - *The originality of Van Gogh's use of the divisionist technique can be seen in this self-portrait of 1887, in which the divided brushstrokes and the color aim for an intensity of expression. Around the face the brushstrokes radiate symbolically, as if they originated from a luminous source.*

XXI - Portrait of Père Tanguy - Athens, Stavros S. Niarchos Coll. - *A friend and admirer of Van Gogh, this modest art and painter's supply dealer was portrayed several times by the artist. This version, painted at the end of 1887, introduces us to the Arles period by the quality of the brushwork and by the intensity of the colors.*

XXII - Sunflowers - New York, The Metropolitan Museum of Art, Rogers Fund 1949 - *Sunflowers were an important theme for Van Gogh, and this canvas of 1887 reflects the research that he had undertaken on dark blues and yellow. But the yellow in this painting, a color that was to constantly reoccur, had not yet exploded with solar intensity as it would under the skies of southern France.*

XXIII - Le Voyer-d'Argenson at Asnières - Private collection - *During the summer of 1887, Van Gogh had the chance to immerse himself in the French countryside. He made trips to the suburbs of Paris, continually observing and annotating, and from this experience he created numerous landscapes. His artistic explorations developed in isolation, however, despite his contact with such artists as Seurat, Signac, and Bernard.*

XXIV-XXV - The Bridge at Langlois - (detail) - Cologne, Wallraf-Richartz Museum - *Open spaces would always have a particular fascination for Van Gogh. He sought depth with a perspective that lost itself in infinity, but at the same time he minutely annotated the elements in the foreground (bridges, roads, etc.) that served as a point of reference and a link for the viewer's eye.*

XXVI - The Bridge of Langlois - Cologne, Wallraf-Richartz Museum - *This painting of May 1888, is perhaps the last version of the subject made by Van Gogh. The small drawbridge is painted in Japanese style, with light and flat colors, but it has an emotional intensity that heralds the works that would be painted during the coming summer.*

XXVII - Boats at Saintes-Maries - Amsterdam, National Museum Vincent Van Gogh - *The visionary emphasis with which Van Gogh interprets reality is revealed in all its power in this beautiful painting made during the summer of 1888, in which the abstract colors gleam and radiate. The expressive quality of these colors is free of any contrived intellectualism.*

XXVIII - Breton Women in a Meadow - Milan, Galleria d'Arte Moderna, raccolta Grassi - *Van Gogh always sought to learn from the works of the old masters as well as those of his contemporaries, assimilating the innovations and discoveries of each. This painting of 1888 is an original interpretation of a work by Emile Bernard, transformed with great expressive freedom by Van Gogh.*

XXIX - Les Alyscamps, Dead Leaves - Otterlo, Kröller-Müller Stichting - *It was inevitable that Van Gogh, obsessed by the expressive values of color, would admire painters who constructed space by the use of bold, arbitrary colors. In this painting of 1888, the revolutionary chromatic lesson of Gauguin dominates the work.*

XXX-XXXI - Houses at Saintes-Maries - U.S.A., private collection - *In the luminous atmosphere of southern France Van Gogh's colors became pure and intense and his drawing simpler. He seems to create a harmonious fusion with nature and the landscape under the skies of Provence that was for him, a natural reflection of his profound spiritual yearning.*

XXXII - Farm in Provence - Amsterdam, Rijksmuseum - *Van Gogh's drawings are preparatory works to be transformed on the canvas, but they are always so complete in themselves that they indicate the high level of expressive mastery he had attained. Many of his drawings, such as this one of 1888, were of landscapes.*

XXXIII - View of an Industrial City - Amsterdam, Stedelijk Museum - *In this painting of 1887, Van Gogh, with his manner of creating a perspective that flows toward the infinite, and with a foreground painted with such intense feeling of the earth, houses, and farm implements, has not yet exploded with that chromatic brilliance that was to emerge during the following summer.*

XXXIV-XXXV - The Plain of La Crau - Amsterdam, National Museum Vincent Van Gogh - *In Arles, Van Gogh, terminating the experiences that had matured in Paris in the use of luminous colors and a brushstroke that built up the image, depicted, during the summer of 1888, the sun-drenched landscape of Provence that was to remain one of the most stimulating elements for his creative fantasy.*

XXXVI - Summer Evening - Winterthur, Kunstmuseum - *With the coming of summer Van Gogh's colors exploded with brilliance. He had discovered the Mediterranean and the fields covered with maturing crops, and all those blues and yellows were to have a fascination for him. In this painting, finished at the end of June, he consciously accumulated the intense colors for it seemed to him that, "night was even richer of colors than the day."*

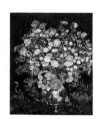

XXXVII - Wildflowers in a Vase - U.S.A., private collection - *The date of this painting is uncertain, but almost all critics think it was made in 1888, due to the evident chromatic research, the study of the various tones of color, and their juxtaposition on the canvas which accords with his maturing artistic evolution of that year.*

XXXVIII - La Mousmé - Washington, National Gallery of Art, Chester Dale Collection - *This portrait of 1888, with its luminous tones, is a delicate and lyrical image in which Van Gogh recapitulates and interprets in an original manner the influence of Japanese prints. With their typical juxtaposition of areas of colors they had a profound influence on him.*

XXXIX - Night Café: Exterior - Otterlo, Kröller-Müller Stichting - *Beneath the stars that shine like a far away salvation, the disquieting light of the café attracts and seduces with the menace of a certain perdition that is frighteningly close. The symbolic concept that upholds the work is realized with a truth that is immediate and direct. This work, painted in 1888, is one of Van Gogh's most important.*

XL-XLI - Night Café: Interior - New Haven, Yale University Art Gallery, Bequest of Stephen Carlton Clark - *Wrote Van Gogh, "I have attempted to show that the café is a place where a man can ruin himself, become mad, commit a crime... I have tried to express the terrible human passions through the use of red and green." The work is dated September 1888.*

XLII - Chair and Pipe - London, Tate Gallery - *The Arles period undoubtedly remains the most important for Van Gogh's artistic activity—during those years he painted the majority of his masterpieces. This canvas of December 1888, shows how even the simplest object, can be charged with meaning through the use of color.*

XLIII - Van Gogh's Bedroom - Amsterdam, National Museum Vincent Van Gogh - *As in the two versions of the Night Café, through the use of contrasting colors and accented brushstrokes, the intimate and luminous harmony of this painting done in the same period suggests a sense of tranquility and repose.*

XLIV - Portrait of Armand Roulin - Essen, Folkwang Museum - *Painted during Gauguin's stay at Arles in November 1888, this portrait shows how Van Gogh was able to find tones of lyrical serenity and human sympathy for people he liked. The Roulin family, in fact, were among the few people with whom the artist had made friends.*

XLV - Reader of Novels - England, private collection - *Painted in November 1888, this canvas demonstrates how the most banal theme was transformed by Van Gogh through his understanding of the underlying significance and its inner meaning and by the use of specific colors that penetrated the simple appearance of things.*

XLVI - Still Life with Onions and Drawing Board - Otterlo, Kröller-Müller Stichting - *The originality of Van Gogh's paintings lies not only in the expressivity of his colors, which he used as a personal language, but in the creation of certain compositional ideas as well. In this painting of January 1889, the subject, seen obliquely, is much more alive and animated than if it were seen frontally.*

XLVII - Vase with Sunflowers - Amsterdam, National Museum Vincent Van Gogh - *With the "sunflower" series, the artist decorated the interior of the small yellow house that he had rented at Arles. In this painting of January 1889, the excitement of the colors attains an almost hallucinatory intensity due to their reduction to a dominant tonality that varies only in luminosity.*

XLVIII - The Postman Joseph Roulin - Otterlo, Kröller-Müller Stichting - *This work was painted during the first few months of 1889, when Van Gogh's paintings achieved their most intense luminosity. The dramatic break with Gauguin was a great shock, but as he himself wrote, his equilibrium as a painter, "was not even grazed." This portrait of his friend Roulin testifies to Van Gogh's intact expressive force.*

XLIX - "La Berceuse" - U.S.A., private collection - *Following the dramatic days, Christmas 1888, of Van Gogh's crisis with Gauguin, the only friendly care and kindness he received was from the Roulin family. In January 1889, he made several portraits of Madame Augustine Roulin, such as this one, in which his mastery of color was affirmed.*

L - Two Cypresses - New York, The Metropolitan Museum of Art, Rogers Fund 1949 - *This painting dates from the period when Van Gogh began his stay at the asylum at Saint-Rémy in June 1889. The emotional tension of the artist is expressed, besides the colors, by the convulsed rhythm of the brushstrokes that seem to shake the cypresses and make the sky tremble.*

LI - Wheatfield with Cypresses - London, National Gallery - *Van Gogh's pictorial and spiritual evolution at Saint-Rémy made him conscious of the basic rhythms of nature that surrounded him. In this painting of 1889, the undulating lines of every element in the landscape define the tumult of the painter's soul.*

LII - Oleanders in the Garden of the Asylum of Saint-Paul - U.S.A., private collection - *This watercolor executed at Saint-Rémy in 1890, is among the works Van Gogh made that returned to his favorite themes. In this angle of the garden the forms and colors seem to soften in the painful search for a moment of serenity.*

LIII - Her Husband Is at Sea - Private collection - *During his stay at Saint-Rémy Van Gogh ordered a large number of books and documents that served both to distract him and to stimulate his imagination. This explains some of the unusual themes found in his paintings, such as this one which was taken from a reproduction of a painting L'homme est en mer, by Virginie Demont-Breton.*

LIV - Self-Portrait with a Cut Ear - London, Courtauld Institute Galleries - *Van Gogh painted this work shortly after the dramatic crisis that ended his friendship with Gauguin. In this painting, as in the similar and more famous one of the self-portrait with the cut ear and pipe, he depicts himself as strangely serene and almost indifferent.*

LV - "L'Arlésienne" - Otterlo, Kröller-Müller Stichting - *It is interesting to compare the two portraits of Madame Ginoux: the first, painted at Arles in 1888, was an explosion of intense colors, expressly emphasized; in this second portrait, made at Saint-Rémy at the beginning of 1890 and inspired by a drawing of Gauguin, the colors are subdued and the focus of the painting is on the expression of the face.*

LVI - Cypresses with Two Female Figures - Otterlo, Kröller-Müller Stichting - *Van Gogh's constant longing for a fusion with nature made him exalt the Arles countryside, with explosions of colors. This painting, made in 1889 or 1890 during a difficult psychological period, reflected his longing in the somber shadows of the cypresses that resemble enormous flames.*

LVII - Road with Cypresses and Stars - Otterlo, Kröller-Müller Stichting - *In this nocturnal landscape of May 1890, we find the unity of inspiration with the other works of the Saint-Rémy period that Van Gogh had never before attained. The details are disregarded in order to underly the whirling rhythms that envelop all things.*

LVIII - Thatched Cottages at Cordeville - Paris, Musée du Louvre - *The last period that Van Gogh passed at Auvers-sur-Oise, from May 1890 on, is a very troubled one, as can be seen in the landscapes painted during the last months. They reflect his dramatic torment, as in this painting in which a whirlwind has stirred all of nature.*

LIX - Chestnut Blossoms - Zurich, Stiftung Sammlung, E.G. Bührle - *This is one of the first painting that Van Gogh made at Auvers. He is still fascinated by nature, and his compositional ability continued to mature. But knowing the significance that he gave to each color, one can detected here the sense of his inner tragedy.*

LX - Self-Portrait - Paris, Musée du Louvre, Jeu de Paume - *In this self-portrait, done during his most anguished period, from 1889 to 1890 at the asylum of Saint-Rémy, Van Gogh expressed the transformation that he underwent by substituting the intense solar colors of his previous paintings with the muffled tones of his solitude.*

LXI - Portrait of Dr. Gachet - Paris, Musée du Louvre, Gachet bequest - *"I would like to paint portraits," wrote Van Gogh, "that in a hundred years from now would appear to their viewers as apparitions." This painting, done a few months before his death, is a vision of his friend who stands out against an intense blue background with a weary expression.*

LXII - Vase with Carnations and Gillyflowers - U.S.A., private collection - *When Van Gogh had painted his bedroom, he wrote to his brother Theo that the yellow color that dominated the painting suggested a "sense of repose." In this painting of 1890, yellow has disappeared and there remains only cold tonalities.*

LXIII - Wheatfield with Crows - Amsterdam, National Museum Vincent Van Gogh - *In the two months at Auvers, Van Gogh produced 70 paintings alternating between landscapes which expressed his desire for inner peace, and paintings of an expressive fury that were beyond any control, as in this dramatic work, painted twenty days before his death, which is his cry of anguish.*

15

II

III

IV

V

VI

VIII

X

XII

XIII

XVII

XVIII

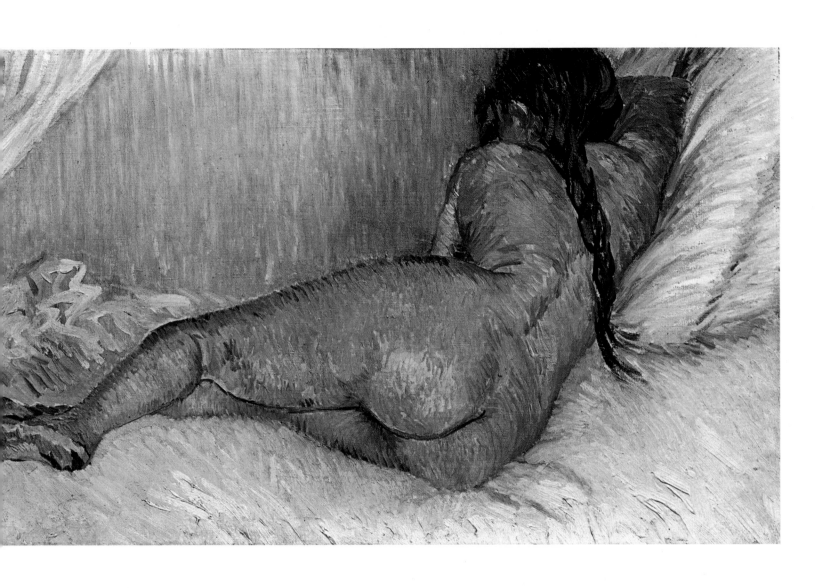

XX

XXII

XXIII

XXIV

d'après un tableau
de É. Bernard

Vincent

XXVIII

XXXI

XXXVI

XXXVIII

XLIV

XLVI

L

LIV

LV

LVIII

LX

LXII

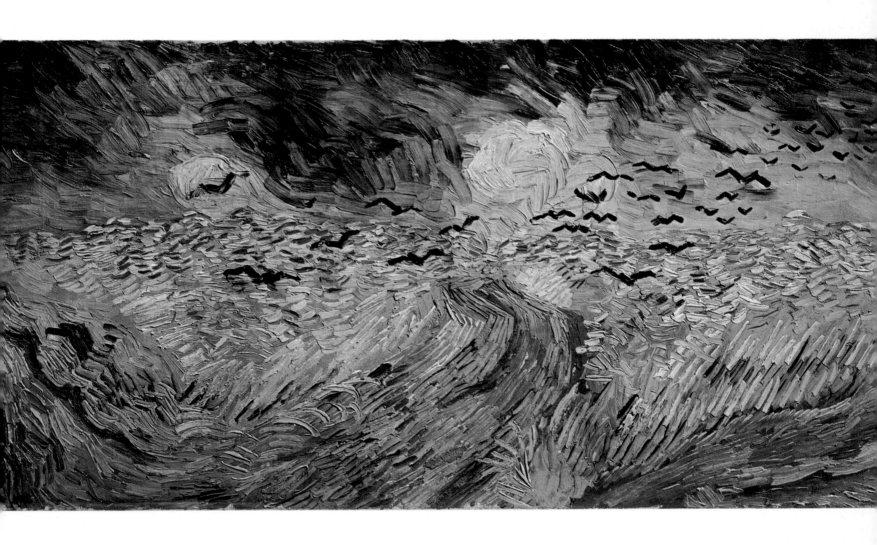

Illustrations from the Picture Archives of Fabbri Editori, Milan
Printed in June 1978, at the graphic plant of Fabbri Editori - Milan, Italy